BE MINDFUL

Developing Self-Awareness

by Ben Hubbard

CAPSTONE PRESS

a capstone imprint

Capstone Captivate is published by Capstone Press, an imprint of Capstone.
1710 Roe Crest Drive
North Mankato, Minnesota 56003
www.capstonepub.com

Library of Congress Cataloging-in-Publication Data is available on the Library of Congress website.
ISBN: 978-1-4966-9522-2 (library binding)
ISBN: 978-1-9771-5386-9 (eBook PDF)

Summary: Whether it's school, extracurricular activities, jobs, or home life, stress and anxiety find ways to overwhelm our minds. It can be easy to get lost in problems. Being mindful and living in the present moment can help. Learn techniques to clear your mind, relax, and shut out distraction. Take the next step to being mindful.

Image Credits
Shutterstock: Aghadhia Studio, 19 bottom, Alla Simacheva, 9, Ami Parikh, 8, AnnGaysorn, 21, Beautiful landscape, 23 top, bubutu, 29, carballo, 10, CGN089, cover, 1, Iconic Bestiary, 11 middle, Iryna Dobrovynska, 19 top, 19 middle, jakkapan, 27, JOKE_PHATRAPONG, 13, joreks, 5, Koval Tetiana, 25, Krakenimages.com, 24, kryzhov, 12, LightField Studios, 14, Lorelyn Medina, 26, mamahoohooba, 20, Monkey Business Images, 4, naulicrea, 29 top, nikiteev_konstantin, 11 bottom, Odua Images, 11 top, Olga Fe, 7, ONYXprj, 15, Rozochkalvn, 18, Samuel Borges Photography, 22, 23 bottom, Sentavio, 17 top, ShvetsovaDesign, 16, SuperBelka, design element, Twinsterphoto, 6, 17 bottom, Victor Brave, 28

Editorial Credits
Editors: Mari Bolte and Alison Deering; Designers: Juliette Peters and Sarah Bennett; Media Researchers: Jo Miller and Tracy Cummins; Production Specialist: Laura Manthe

Table of Contents

Words in **bold** are in the glossary.

What Is Mindfulness?

From dawn to dusk, our days are filled with worries. We worry about being on time. We worry about having the right things with us. We worry about ourselves, and we worry about other people. We spend so much time thinking about our troubles that we can forget to pay attention to what's happening around us.

Trying to keep up with a busy, fast-paced life can leave us thinking about what we did wrong or what comes next. We can spend a lot of time dwelling on the things that worry us. That worry can keep us from thinking of the most important thing—the present.

Take a minute. Breathe deeply. Let your troubles go, at least for a moment. Think about the present moment—the here and now.

Mindfulness means living in the present and being aware of how you are feeling within it. It means accepting what is happening around you and treating it with a patient, calm attitude. Mindfulness can help keep our problems in **perspective**.

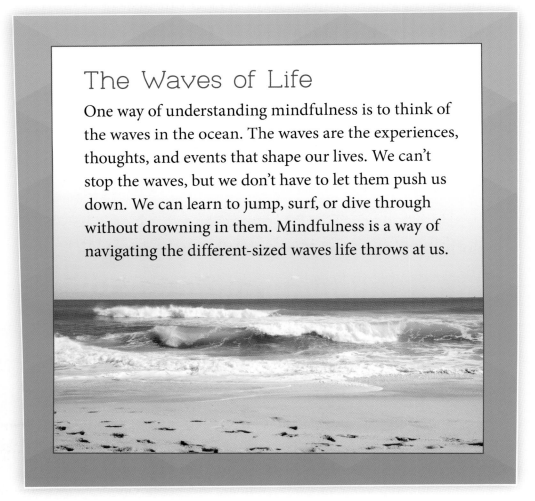

The Waves of Life

One way of understanding mindfulness is to think of the waves in the ocean. The waves are the experiences, thoughts, and events that shape our lives. We can't stop the waves, but we don't have to let them push us down. We can learn to jump, surf, or dive through without drowning in them. Mindfulness is a way of navigating the different-sized waves life throws at us.

Chapter 1

What's on Your Mind?

We have so many thoughts and feelings running through our heads. Sometimes it can feel like you're having an entire conversation. Those voices talk about everything: about how you feel today, about a friend's message this morning, about what you'll have for lunch. Thoughts can be happy, sad, angry, fun, naughty, or worried.

Can I Turn Thoughts Off?

Close your eyes for 20 seconds and think of nothing. Now open your eyes. What happened? Were you able to keep your mind empty and clear of thoughts? If not, don't worry. Most people couldn't. Thoughts are almost impossible to turn off.

Thoughts as Clouds

The problem with thoughts is that they can make our minds busy and affect our moods. We can't get rid of them. But we can let them pass. Imagine your thoughts are clouds drifting overhead. There are so many of them! Don't focus on them. Let them come together into one big cloud. Now let that cloud float away.

What's Worrying You?

It is normal to worry. All of us do it from time to time. It could be caused by small, **trivial** things. But it can also be caused by big things we can't control. There are endless things to worry about. But the result is often the same—we feel nervous, unsure, and lack confidence. How do we get rid of worry?

What if I fail the test?

Out of Your Head

Here's a simple exercise to get rid of worries and concentrate on your breathing. Use it whenever a new worry shows itself.

1. Think of something that's worrying you. Let it swirl around inside your body.

2. Take a long, deep breath through your nose. Imagine that worrying thought being pulled to your body's center.

3. Exhale through your mouth. Push the worry out and away from you.

4. Repeat this exercise through several breath cycles.

Obsessive Thoughts

Some thoughts are more **obsessive** than others. Planning for the weekend, daydreaming about a vacation, or worrying about a test are the kinds of thoughts that don't easily disappear. But that kind of thinking takes us away from what is happening in the present moment. The opposite of being mindful, overthinking can take you out of the moment and make it hard to return.

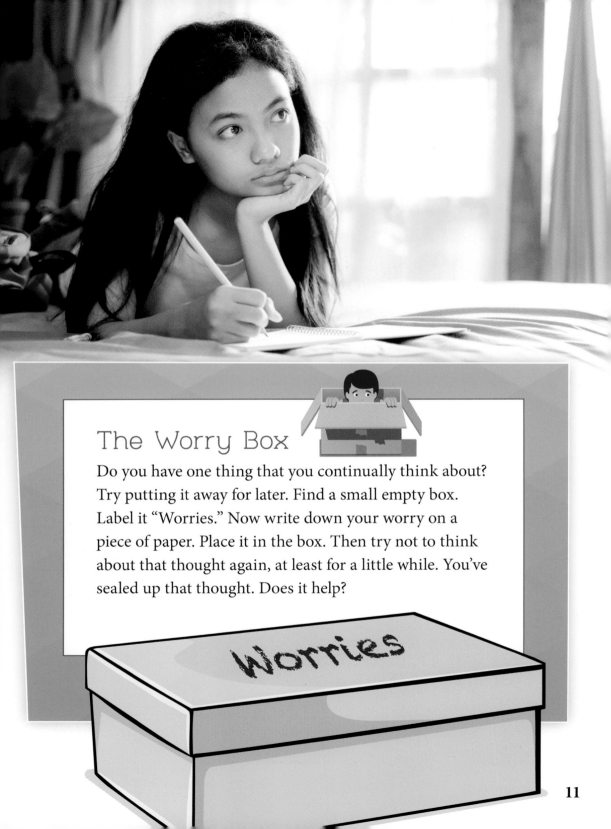

The Worry Box

Do you have one thing that you continually think about? Try putting it away for later. Find a small empty box. Label it "Worries." Now write down your worry on a piece of paper. Place it in the box. Then try not to think about that thought again, at least for a little while. You've sealed up that thought. Does it help?

Worries

Approaching Life

Worrying too much can have a huge effect on how much we enjoy our lives. When we do well, it makes us feel good. When things don't go our way, we feel bad. We can't control those feelings. But we can work on how those feelings affect us.

Being mindful means accepting the things that happen and approaching life with a positive attitude. How do we start?

1. Slow down and notice the things around you. What are five things you haven't noticed in this room before? What do things smell or sound like there?

2. Treat yourself like you treat other people. Be kind and stick up for yourself. You are your harshest **critic**—instead, be your best friend.

3. On that note, treat other people kindly too. Don't hang around people who make you feel bad.

4. If someone or something hurts your feelings, accept how it made you feel, and then try to put it behind you. Dwelling on your hurt feelings just takes you away from moving on.

Technology Distractions

One thing that can take you out of the moment is technology. Phones, video games, televisions, and movies are constant distractions. They can be helpful tools, but they are also tools that should only be used when we really need them.

Digital Detox

How often do you look at your phone? Grab a notebook and make a check mark every time you pick it up over one day. You might be surprised at what you'll learn. Taking a digital **detox** means turning off your phone or setting time limits. Could you do this for a week, a day, or even an afternoon? Give it a try.

The World Wide Web of Distractions

The internet is an amazing way to communicate and find information. But how much time do you waste clicking on random links? Test yourself the next time you're online. Check your browser history to get an accurate picture.

Gaming Black Holes

Gaming can be great, but it can also be a time suck. To stop falling into the "just another five minutes" trap, set an alarm. Switch off the game when the alarm goes off. (No snoozing!)

Chapter 2

How Mindfulness Can Help

We've seen that the world is full of distractions. We know that thoughts and worries can take us away from the present moment. Sometimes all of these things happen at the same time. Sometimes they build up until we reach a breaking point. How can mindfulness help when we get stressed out? Try elevator breathing!

Elevator Breathing

1. Imagine there is an elevator in your body. Your head is the top floor. Your feet are the bottom floor.

2. Breathe in. Then release the breath. As you breathe out, imagine the elevator going from your head to your chest.

3. Pause. Breathe in again. Imagine the doors are opening. Imagine your breath filling the elevator with fresh air.

4. Breathe out. As you do so, imagine the elevator going down to the next floor at your stomach. Repeat step three.

5. Now imagine the elevator going down to the bottom floor, your feet. Repeat step three. How do you feel now?

Follow Your Senses

Did the elevator breathing exercise make you feel calmer? Deep breathing lowers the body's **heart rate**, fills the lungs with oxygen-rich air, and encourages relaxation. But by concentrating on a physical sensation—in this case, your breathing—you were also only involved in what was happening right here, right now. That's because physical sensations such as breathing, hearing, seeing, touching, smelling, and tasting, always take place in the present moment.

The more you are in the present moment, the less likely you are to be concerned by thoughts, worries, or other distractions. That's what being mindful is all about.

Morning Mindfulness

Morning is the best time to start mindfulness. Every action you take is a single step to get you to the next moment.

Pull the bedcovers back.

Sit up.

Get out of bed.

Walk to the bathroom or the closet.

Brush your teeth.

Try not to think too far ahead. By being mindful of each moment as it comes, you are living in the moment and not getting ahead of yourself. Try to stay in that state as long as possible.

Chapter 3

Exercising Mindfulness

With some practice, it's easy to become mindful. Learn the exercises that will teach you how. Then make a point to do those exercises when your mind starts to wander. The first exercise shows you how to concentrate on one sense (in this case, hearing) to bring you into the present moment.

The Hearing Exercise

1. Sit with your back straight and your arms relaxed.

2. Close your eyes. Breathe in. Then exhale, paying attention to the air as it leaves your body.

3. Listen to what you can hear around you. Focus on the first sound you notice. Maybe it's the refrigerator humming, or cars on a nearby road. Give that sound your full attention for at least a few moments.

4. Now listen to the other sounds around you. Choose another sound as your focus.

5. If your mind is interrupted by a thought, tell it you are "listening." Let that thought go.

6. Listen to the sounds for a few minutes and then open your eyes. Do you feel like you were successfully mindful?

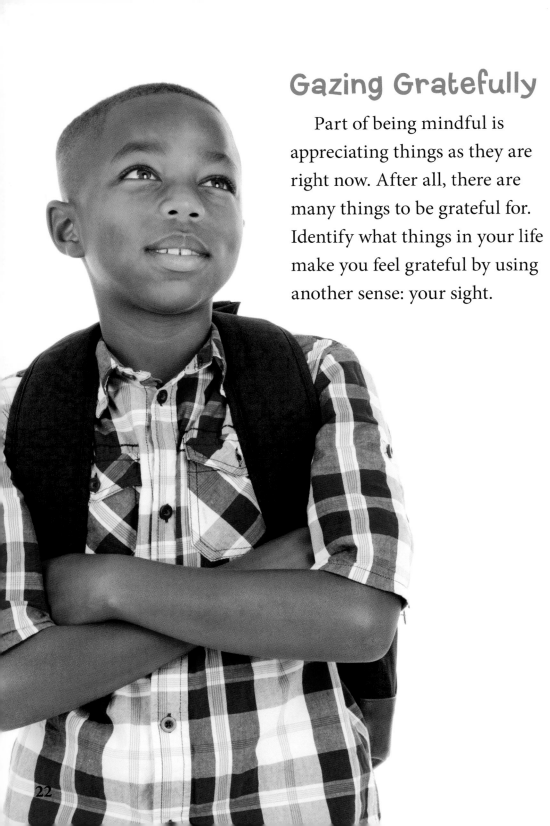

Gazing Gratefully

Part of being mindful is appreciating things as they are right now. After all, there are many things to be grateful for. Identify what things in your life make you feel grateful by using another sense: your sight.

Gazing Gratefully

1. Take a slow, calm breath into your belly.

2. Look at the place you are in. It might be a living room, or bedroom, or somewhere outside.

3. Gaze around you. Name each thing you are grateful for. Is it a favorite mug? A new notebook? A blooming flower?

4. Remember, gazing gratefully is not a test. There is no right or wrong answer. You're the only one who can decide what things make you happy. How do you feel after the exercise?

I'm grateful for the fall leaves I see on my way to school.

Eat Like an Alien

Food is one way we connect ourselves to the world. Whether it's a favorite meal or a new dish, food can bring people together in the present. But sometimes we eat on **autopilot**, not really tasting the food or experiencing the moment. Take the time to sit down and savor your meal! Eating like an alien is an exercise that challenges us to experience food like it's our first time.

Eat Like an Alien

1. Prepare a plate of food. For the first time, try something simple, like cut-up fruit or vegetables.

2. Choose a piece of the food. Look at it like it's the first time you've ever seen it. What color is it? What does it look like? Can you describe its texture?

3. Smell the food. Then put it into your mouth. What does it feel like? Does it taste like it smells?

4. As you chew, observe how it tastes.

Balloon Breathing

How are you progressing with your mindfulness? Have you learned some different **techniques** to stay in the present? It takes time to train yourself to be mindful. Don't be upset if thoughts and feelings creep in. If they become a problem, though, you can imagine sending them off like balloons.

Thought Send-off

1. Sit with your back straight and arms relaxed. Close your eyes.

2. Think of a thought, feeling, or worry that is bothering you.

3. Imagine placing that thought, feeling, or worry in a balloon.

4. Blow up the mental balloon. Tie off the end. Now let it go.

5. Watch the balloon float away into the sky above you.

6. Once it has disappeared, open your eyes. How do you feel now?

Climate change scares me.

What if . . . ?

I can't fall asleep.

I'm worried about people liking me.

My dentist appointment is tomorrow.

I must do better at basketball.

Chapter 4

Mindfulness for the Future

Achieving mindfulness is within your grasp. There are still a few more tips and tricks to getting there.

S.T.O.P.

Stop whatever you are doing.

Take a long, calm breath and concentrate on it going in and out.

Observe what is making you feel stressed out and accept that it is happening.

Proceed with your day now that you've acknowledged what was bothering you.

Did you notice a difference between before and after **STOP**ping? That's what being mindful is all about.

Finger Counting

1. Breathe in. Make a fist as you do.

2. Breathe out. Straighten your thumb as you let out the air. Breathe in.

3. Breathe out and unbend your index finger. Breathe in.

4. Continue in this way until all your fingers are straight. How do you feel now? Hopefully calm and back in the present moment.

Glossary

autopilot (AW-toh-py-luht)—to do something automatically, without thinking

critic (KRIT-ik)—a person who finds fault or complains

detox (DEE-toks)—to take a break from something

heart rate (HART RAYT)—the number of heartbeats per minute

obsessive (uhb-SES-iv)—thinking about something or someone too much or in a way that is not normal

perspective (per-SPEK-tiv)—an accurate rating of what is important and what isn't

technique (tek-NEEK)—a method or a way of doing something that requires skill

trivial (TRIV-ee-uhl)—of little worth or importance

Read More

Andrus, Aubre and Karen Bluth. *Happiness Hacks: How to Find Energy and Inspiration*. North Mankato, MN: Capstone Press, 2018.

Falligant, Erin. *A Smart Girl's Guide: Getting It Together: How to Organize Your Space, Your Stuff, Your Time—and Your Life*. Middleton, WI: American Girl Publishing, 2017.

Sargent, Kristina. *Mindful Games For Kids: 50 Fun Activities to Stay Present, Improve Concentration, and Understand Emotions*. Emeryville, CA: Rockridge Press, 2019.

Internet Sites

Mindfulness
kidshealth.org/en/kids/mindfulness.html

Relax & Unwind Center
kidshealth.org/en/kids/center/relax-center.html?WT.ac=k-nav-relax-center

Mindfulness Exercises
kidshealth.org/en/kids/mindful-exercises.html?WT.ac=k-ra

Index